The True Story of Maggie Smith

A complete biography of the British actress, her early life, career, relationship, health challenges and the narrative of her passing

Saraline Tusks

Copyright © 2024 by Saraline Tusks

All rights reserved. No part of this publication may be reproduced, distributed, or transmitted in any form or by any means, including photocopying, recording, or other electronic or mechanical methods, without the prior written permission of the publisher, except in the case of brief quotations embodied in critical reviews and certain other noncommercial uses permitted by copyright law

Table of Contents

INTRODUCTION 5

    A Summary of Maggie Smith's Contributions 5

CHAPTER 1: Early Life and Background 10

    Childhood and Family Life 10

    Education and Early Interests 13

    Discovering the Passion for Acting 16

CHAPTER 2: The Rise to Stardom 21

    Early Career: Theatrical Beginnings 21

    Breakthrough Roles in Film and Television 24

    Notable Performances and Awards 28

CHAPTER 3: Relationships and Personal Life 32

    Marriage and Family Dynamics 32

    Friendships and Collaborations in the Industry 35

    Navigating Love and Heartbreak 38

CHAPTER 4: Health Challenges and Resilience 43

    Struggles with Illness: A Personal Journey 43

    Coping Mechanisms and Support Systems 46

    Impact on Career and Public Life 49

CHAPTER 5: Later Career and Continued Influence...

    Iconic Roles in Later Years..........................54

    Contributions to Theatre and Film......................57

    Legacy and Influence on New Generations of Actors..................61

CHAPTER 6: The Narrative of Her Passing..............66

    Circumstances Surrounding Her Death................ 66

    Public Reactions and Tributes...............................68

    Reflection on Her Life and Impact........................70

CONCLUSION..73

INTRODUCTION

A Summary of Maggie Smith's Contributions

Dame Maggie Smith has left her stamp on the annals of cinematic history. Her name is a byword for ability, grace, and perseverance. With a career spanning more than seven decades, Smith's many roles in theater, film, and television have enthralled audiences all over the world. She is one of the most renowned actors of her time because of her performances, which are distinguished by a special wit and depth combination. From her first days on stage to her well-known performances in movies like *The Prime of Miss Jean Brodie* and the adored *Harry Potter* series, Smith's career is a monument to both her extraordinary talent and her significant influence on the arts.

Smith, who was born in Essex, England, in 1934, showed a talent for acting at a young age. Her spectacular career began with her official schooling at the Oxford Playhouse. Early in the 1950s, she made her professional debut and rose to prominence in British theater. She had an unmatched presence on stage and was well-received by critics for her ability to embody nuanced roles. Smith's adaptability made it easy for her to go from the stage to the movie, where she was a successful leading woman.

Smith's performance in *The Prime of Miss Jean Brodie* cemented her reputation as a formidable actress who could take on difficult parts in addition to winning her an Academy Award. Her signature style of expressing profound emotional truths was on full display in this performance. She has been recognized with many honors during her career, including several nominations for Golden Globe Awards and BAFTA Awards, which attest to her outstanding contributions to the performing arts.

The secret to Smith's legacy is not just her amazing resume but also her ability to portray audiences with strong, multidimensional characters that they can relate to. Pop culture has been forever impacted by characters like Violet Crawley, the Dowager Countess of Grantham in *Downton Abbey*, and Professor Minerva McGonagall in the *Harry Potter* series. These parts highlight her ability to give her characters warmth and insight, which makes them memorable and approachable.

Maggie Smith's influence goes beyond the big screen. Her commitment to her work and her unbreakable spirit in the face of personal adversity have inspired numerous young actors and actresses. Fans view her as more relatable as a result of her open difficulties with health issues, especially her fight with breast cancer, which have demonstrated her perseverance. Smith has positively impacted society by using her platform to promote worthy causes like education and the arts.

Smith's dedication to theater, where she still performs and coaches up-and-coming artists, adds even more value to her legacy. Her performances in Shakespearean parts, in particular, have raised the bar for quality and artistry in British theater. She is further solidifying her place as a cultural icon as other actresses credit her with having had a major influence on their careers.

It becomes clear as we learn more about Maggie Smith's life and work that it's not just a tale of success and recognition but also one of tenacity, passion, and the enduring power of art. She has pushed boundaries, confronted social standards, and given voice to women's realities through her performances. Her legacy is a multicolored tapestry made from the strands of her many successes and the lives she has impacted. By honoring Maggie Smith, we not only pay tribute to her accomplishments to the performing industry but also to the lasting impact she has made on culture, encouraging future generations to follow their ambitions with courage and grace.

CHAPTER 1: Early Life and Background

Childhood and Family Life

Dame Maggie Smith was born on December 28, 1934, in Essex, England, to a family that would play a crucial role in shaping her early experiences and interests. She was the daughter of Margaret Hutton, a Scottish woman, and William Smith, a naval officer. Maggie was raised in a nurturing environment, where creativity and the arts were encouraged. The Smith household was filled with love and support, fostering her early inclinations toward performance and storytelling.

Growing up in a modest home, Smith's family life was influenced by the values of hard work and resilience. Her father, often away due to his naval commitments, instilled a sense of discipline and responsibility in Maggie and her siblings. Despite the challenges of having a father frequently absent, Smith maintained a close relationship with her mother, who was instrumental in introducing her to the arts. Her mother's passion for theatre and literature provided a backdrop for Maggie's own burgeoning interests. Family gatherings often included lively discussions about books and plays, sparking Maggie's imagination and desire to engage with the world of storytelling.

From a young age, Smith exhibited an inclination towards the performing arts. Her family often attended local theatre productions, where Maggie first experienced the magic of live performances. The bright lights of the stage captivated her, and she was enchanted by the ability of actors to transport audiences into different worlds. It was during these formative years that she began to dream of a career in acting.

Despite the warmth of her home life, Smith faced challenges typical of many children. She was a shy girl, often finding solace in her imagination and the characters she created in her mind. This duality of being introverted while yearning for the spotlight would become a defining feature of her personality. The supportive nature of her family helped her navigate these early insecurities, allowing her to explore her interests freely.

Maggie's childhood was also marked by the impact of World War II. Growing up during this tumultuous period influenced her worldview and instilled in her a sense of empathy that would later inform her performances. The war brought a level of uncertainty and hardship, and Maggie witnessed the strength and resilience of her mother and other women in her community. This experience deepened her understanding of human emotion, providing a rich reservoir of inspiration for her future work as an actress.

As Smith transitioned into adolescence, her desire to perform became more pronounced. The support of her family remained pivotal, encouraging her to pursue her passions even when she faced challenges. The nurturing environment of her childhood laid a solid foundation for her eventual journey into the world of acting, preparing her to embrace both the triumphs and tribulations that lay ahead.

Education and Early Interests

Maggie Smith's educational journey was characterized by a blend of formal schooling and artistic exploration. After attending a local primary school, she was accepted into the prestigious North London Collegiate School. It was here that her interest in acting truly began to flourish. The school provided a robust academic environment alongside opportunities for creative expression, and Smith took full advantage of both.

At North London Collegiate, Maggie participated in various school plays, which allowed her to hone her craft and discover her unique voice as an actress.

Her teachers recognized her talent early on and encouraged her to pursue drama as a serious career. This affirmation from her educators, coupled with her burgeoning confidence, fueled her passion for the performing arts. Smith developed a love for literature and began to immerse herself in the works of playwrights such as Shakespeare, understanding the complexity of characters and the power of words.

Maggie's education extended beyond the classroom as she sought to engage with the vibrant cultural scene in London. She attended theatre productions, immersing herself in the performances of established actors and absorbing the nuances of stagecraft. This exposure not only broadened her understanding of acting but also ignited a desire to be part of that world. Smith was particularly influenced by the post-war revival of British theatre, where innovation and experimentation were at the forefront.

After completing her schooling, she pursued further education at the Oxford Playhouse, where she received formal training in acting. This pivotal step allowed her to refine her skills, explore various techniques, and gain valuable experience in performance. The Oxford Playhouse was a breeding ground for emerging talent, and Smith thrived in this environment, collaborating with fellow students and experienced professionals. She was known for her dedication and work ethic, attributes that would serve her well throughout her career.

Maggie's early interests were not confined to acting alone; she was also fascinated by literature, particularly poetry. Her love for language deepened her understanding of character development and dialogue. She often found inspiration in the written word, using poetry as a means of expressing her emotions and exploring the intricacies of human relationships. This intellectual curiosity enriched her performances and provided her with a diverse palette from which to draw.

Despite her growing ambitions, Smith faced challenges during her educational journey. The competitive nature of the arts meant that she often encountered setbacks and rejections. However, her resilience and determination to succeed propelled her forward. With the unwavering support of her family, she persevered, embracing every opportunity to learn and grow as an actress.

Discovering the Passion for Acting

Maggie Smith's passion for acting did not merely emerge overnight; it was a gradual process shaped by various influences and experiences throughout her formative years. Her initial exposure to the stage ignited a spark within her, but it was the culmination of her education, family support, and personal exploration that ultimately led her to embrace acting as her lifelong vocation.

As a teenager, Maggie's involvement in school productions provided her with her first taste of performance. Each role she played was a chance to explore different facets of her personality and gain insight into the human condition. These early performances became more than just exercises in acting; they were opportunities for self-discovery and personal growth. Through her characters, she learned to navigate the complexities of emotion and empathy, skills that would become hallmarks of her illustrious career.

Maggie's dedication to the craft intensified during her time at the Oxford Playhouse. Immersed in a world of creativity and artistic expression, she found herself surrounded by like-minded individuals who shared her passion for acting. This community of aspiring artists inspired her to push boundaries and delve deeper into her performances. The atmosphere was charged with a sense of possibility, and Smith relished the opportunity to experiment and refine her skills under the guidance of experienced mentors.

While at Oxford, Smith was introduced to various acting techniques and styles, from classical to contemporary. She began to develop her unique approach to character work, drawing inspiration from the characters she encountered in literature and theatre. The fusion of her academic background and practical experience allowed her to craft nuanced performances that resonated with audiences on multiple levels.

Maggie's breakthrough moment came when she landed her first professional role in a theatre production shortly after graduating from Oxford. The experience solidified her commitment to acting as a career. It was a transformative moment that reaffirmed her love for the craft, and she realized that performing was not merely a passion but her calling.

As she navigated the early stages of her career, Smith faced numerous challenges and uncertainties typical of aspiring actors. The competitive landscape of the entertainment industry was daunting, but her passion fueled her perseverance. She embraced every audition and opportunity with tenacity, often drawing strength from the supportive foundation her family had provided. Their belief in her potential helped her weather the inevitable disappointments, allowing her to focus on honing her craft.

Maggie's early experiences in the industry taught her valuable lessons about resilience and adaptability. Each role, regardless of size, contributed to her growth as an actress. She approached her work with a sense of curiosity, viewing every character as a chance to explore new aspects of herself. This thirst for discovery became a defining feature of her artistic journey.

Through her unwavering dedication and passion for acting, Maggie Smith emerged as a formidable talent, ready to leave her mark on the world. The combination of her rich background, supportive family, and early experiences in theatre laid the groundwork for a remarkable career, one that would ultimately lead her to become a beloved icon in the entertainment industry. Her story serves as a testament to the transformative power of art and the impact of nurturing one's passions from a young age.

CHAPTER 2: The Rise to Stardom

Early Career: Theatrical Beginnings

Maggie Smith's rise to stardom began in the heart of British theatre, where her talent was nurtured and developed through a series of pivotal performances. After graduating from the Oxford Playhouse, Smith embarked on her professional career in the early 1950s. Her first significant role came in the 1952 production of "The Country Girls," where she showcased her impressive range and ability to bring complex characters to life. This initial exposure to the theatrical world marked the beginning of a journey that would see her become one of the most revered actresses in the industry.

In the years that followed, Maggie honed her craft by taking on various roles in regional theatres and London's West End. Each performance was an opportunity for her to refine her skills and develop a unique stage presence. She quickly gained recognition for her ability to convey deep emotion, often playing strong, complex female characters. Critics lauded her performances, noting her exceptional ability to transition seamlessly between comedy and drama.

Maggie's theatrical journey continued with a series of notable productions, including her portrayal of Helena in Shakespeare's "A Midsummer Night's Dream" and her role in "The Prime of Miss Jean Brodie." These performances not only showcased her versatility but also solidified her status as a leading actress in the theatre scene. The latter role, in particular, would later define her career, as it earned her significant acclaim and set the stage for her transition into film and television.

The early years of **Smith's** career were characterized by a deep commitment to her craft. She often collaborated with renowned directors and playwrights, immersing herself in the rich tradition of British theatre. This dedication to live performance allowed her to develop a distinct style, marked by emotional depth and authenticity. Audiences were drawn to her performances, captivated by her ability to portray characters with remarkable nuance.

Smith's work in the theatre not only established her as a formidable talent but also provided her with valuable connections within the entertainment industry. It was during this period that she began to attract the attention of film and television producers, paving the way for her eventual breakthrough into the cinematic realm. The foundation she built on stage would prove invaluable as she transitioned into film, where her theatrical training would serve her well in the nuanced world of screen acting.

In 1961, Maggie made her film debut in "The Honeysuckle and the Bear," a comedy that marked the beginning of her journey into the world of cinema. Though her film career initially took a backseat to her theatrical pursuits, her early experiences in the industry laid the groundwork for what was to come. As she continued to refine her craft on stage, it became increasingly clear that her talent was not limited to theatre alone. The stage had prepared her for the challenges and opportunities that awaited her in film and television.

The 1960s proved to be a turning point for Smith as she garnered critical acclaim for her performances, ultimately earning her a reputation as one of the leading actresses of her generation. Her early career in theatre set the stage for a successful transition into film and television, where her talent would shine even brighter.

Breakthrough Roles in Film and Television

Maggie Smith's transition from the stage to the screen was marked by a series of breakthrough roles that showcased her exceptional talent and versatility as an actress. In the early 1970s, she gained widespread recognition for her portrayal of Jean Brodie in the film adaptation of "The Prime of Miss Jean Brodie," directed by Ronald Neame. The role, originally crafted for the stage, became a defining moment in her career and earned her the Academy Award for Best Actress in 1970. This remarkable achievement catapulted Smith into the spotlight, establishing her as one of the leading actresses in the industry.

Following her success in "The Prime of Miss Jean Brodie," Maggie continued to secure high-profile roles that highlighted her unique ability to bring complex characters to life. In 1972, she starred in "Travels with My Aunt," directed by George Cukor, where she played the eccentric Aunt Augusta. Her performance was met with critical acclaim, and she received another Academy Award nomination for Best Actress. This film showcased Smith's remarkable comedic timing and ability to embody quirky characters, further solidifying her reputation as a versatile actress.

Smith's breakthrough in film was complemented by her success on television. In the 1970s and 1980s, she appeared in several acclaimed miniseries and television films, including "The Deadly Affair" and "The Approach." Her work in television allowed her to reach a broader audience, and she became a familiar face to viewers around the world. One of her most notable television roles came in the acclaimed series "Downton Abbey," which premiered in 2010. As the formidable Dowager Countess Violet Crawley, Smith captivated audiences with her sharp wit and impeccable comedic timing. This role introduced her to a new generation of fans and reaffirmed her status as a beloved figure in the entertainment industry.

As her career progressed, Smith continued to take on diverse roles across various genres, showcasing her remarkable range. In 1987, she starred in "A

Room with a View," a period drama directed by James Ivory, where she played the role of Charlotte Bartlett. Her performance garnered critical acclaim and contributed to the film's success, further establishing her as a leading actress in both film and television.

Maggie Smith's ability to navigate between dramatic and comedic roles became a hallmark of her career. Her performances were characterized by a depth of emotion and an authenticity that resonated with audiences. With each new project, she continued to push boundaries, proving her versatility and adaptability in a constantly evolving industry.

By the late 20th century, Maggie Smith had firmly established herself as a cinematic icon. Her breakthrough roles not only showcased her talent but also contributed to the evolution of female characters in film and television. She became known for portraying strong, independent women who defied societal norms and expectations. This legacy of empowered female characters would continue to inspire future generations of actresses.

Notable Performances and Awards

Maggie Smith's career is adorned with numerous notable performances that have left an indelible mark on the entertainment industry. Her ability to inhabit a diverse array of characters with grace and authenticity has earned her critical acclaim and a dedicated fan base. Over the years, Smith has received numerous awards and accolades, cementing her status as one of the most respected actresses of her generation.

One of her most celebrated performances came in the film "The Prime of Miss Jean Brodie," where she portrayed the unconventional teacher with a radical approach to education. The role not only garnered her an Academy Award but also showcased her ability to balance complexity and charisma in her performances. Critics praised her portrayal, noting how she brought depth to a character who could easily have been one-dimensional. This performance marked a pivotal moment in her career, establishing her as a leading actress in both film and theatre.

In addition to her Academy Award, Smith has received several BAFTA Awards, which recognize excellence in British film and television. Her performance in "The Prime of Miss Jean Brodie" earned her a BAFTA, and she would go on to win additional awards for her work in films such as "A Room with a View" and "The Lonely Passion of Judith Hearne." These accolades reflected her remarkable range and ability to captivate audiences across different genres.

Throughout her career, Maggie Smith has also been recognized for her contributions to the theatre. In 1976, she received the prestigious Olivier Award for her performance in the play "The Lady from the Sea," directed by Richard Eyre. This award, named after the legendary actor Laurence Olivier, is one of the highest honors in British theatre and is a testament to Smith's enduring impact on the stage.

As her career progressed into the 21st century, Maggie continued to earn accolades for her work. Her portrayal of the Dowager Countess in "Downton Abbey" not only resonated with audiences but also garnered her a Screen Actors Guild Award for Outstanding Performance by an Ensemble in a Drama Series. The character became a cultural phenomenon, known for her sharp wit and memorable one-liners, further solidifying Smith's place in the hearts of viewers worldwide.

In 2015, Maggie Smith was honored with the prestigious BAFTA Fellowship, recognizing her outstanding contribution to film and television. This accolade is reserved for individuals who have made a significant impact on the industry, and Smith's extensive body of work undoubtedly exemplifies that legacy.

Beyond the accolades and awards, Maggie Smith's performances have left a lasting influence on both her peers and aspiring actors. She has become a role model for many, demonstrating the power of authenticity in acting. Her commitment to her craft and her ability to convey profound emotions have inspired countless actresses to pursue their dreams and strive for excellence in their performances.

Maggie Smith's notable performances and the recognition she has received throughout her career are a testament to her talent and dedication to the art of acting. Her ability to portray complex characters across various mediums has solidified her status as a cultural icon, ensuring that her legacy will endure for generations to come. From her theatrical beginnings to her celebrated roles in film and television, Smith's journey is a remarkable narrative of artistry and achievement.

CHAPTER 3: Relationships and Personal Life

Marriage and Family Dynamics

Maggie Smith's personal life, particularly her experiences with marriage and family dynamics, reflects the complexities of balancing a demanding career with personal relationships. Born in 1934 in Essex, England, Maggie Smith was the daughter of a Scottish father and a mother who worked as a secretary. She was raised in a nurturing environment that encouraged her artistic pursuits, yet the realities of her professional life would eventually present challenges in her relationships.

In 1956, Maggie Smith married actor Robert Stephens, whom she met while performing at the Oxford Playhouse. Their union was marked by shared artistic aspirations; both were deeply involved in theatre and film, which initially fostered a strong bond between them. They welcomed two sons, Toby and Chris, during their marriage. However, as Maggie's career took off, the dynamics within their family began to shift. With her increasing prominence in the entertainment industry, the pressures of fame and work commitments began to strain their relationship.

While both Maggie and Robert were talented actors, their careers often demanded long hours and extensive travel, which made maintaining a stable family life challenging. The tension between their professional lives and personal commitments culminated in their separation in 1975, followed by their divorce in 1980. Despite the challenges they faced as a couple, Maggie and Robert remained committed to co-parenting their children. Their dedication to their sons ensured that family bonds remained intact, even as they navigated the complexities of their individual careers.

Following her divorce from Robert Stephens, Maggie Smith entered into a long-term relationship with playwright Beverley Cross. The couple had a deep connection, bonded by their love for the arts and mutual respect for each other's talents. They married in 1975, and their partnership flourished, allowing Maggie to find a sense of stability amidst the tumult of her professional life. Cross's support was crucial, particularly during the later years of Maggie's career when she faced health challenges. Their relationship was marked by a shared understanding of the pressures of the entertainment industry, and they enjoyed a profound companionship until Cross's passing in 2008.

Maggie Smith's approach to her family life demonstrates a commitment to nurturing her relationships, even amidst the challenges posed by her career. Her ability to adapt and maintain a strong sense of family, despite her personal hardships, reflects her resilience and dedication.

Smith often emphasized the importance of her sons in her life, sharing anecdotes of their upbringing and the joys of motherhood. The warmth and love she fostered within her family remain an integral part of her identity, grounding her amidst the ever-changing landscape of her career.

Friendships and Collaborations in the Industry

Maggie Smith's career has been defined not only by her extraordinary talent but also by the friendships and collaborations she has cultivated within the entertainment industry. Throughout her long and illustrious career, Smith has formed meaningful relationships with numerous actors, directors, and playwrights, each contributing to her artistic journey and enriching her experiences in the industry.

One of the most significant friendships in Maggie Smith's career was with fellow actress Judi Dench. The two shared a close bond, often supporting one another through the ups and downs of their respective careers. Their friendship is rooted in mutual respect for each other's talent and a shared passion for acting. Dench and Smith have often expressed admiration for one another, celebrating each other's successes and offering comfort during challenging times. This camaraderie is a testament to the supportive nature of their relationship, which has endured through decades in the spotlight.

Collaboration has also played a pivotal role in Smith's career. Her work with esteemed directors, such as Mike Leigh and James Ivory, has led to some of her most memorable performances. Leigh's innovative approach to storytelling allowed Smith to explore her characters deeply, resulting in nuanced portrayals that captivated audiences. Similarly, her collaboration with Ivory on films like "A Room with a View" showcased her ability to thrive in diverse genres while forming strong professional bonds. These collaborations have not only advanced her career but have also fostered lasting friendships within the industry.

Maggie Smith's work on "Downton Abbey" introduced her to a new generation of actors, many of whom became friends and collaborators. The ensemble cast developed strong bonds while working together, creating a supportive environment that facilitated creativity and artistic expression. Smith's interactions with her co-stars, particularly Michelle Dockery and Hugh Bonneville, exemplified the spirit of camaraderie that often flourishes in ensemble productions. Their shared experiences and collective dedication to the show contributed to the overall success of the series, highlighting the importance of collaboration in Smith's career.

Moreover, her relationships with playwrights and screenwriters have been instrumental in shaping her career trajectory. Maggie's connections with writers, such as Alan Ayckbourn and David Mamet, allowed her to explore diverse roles that challenged her as an actress. Their collaborative efforts resulted in some of her most memorable performances, further solidifying her reputation as a versatile and talented actress.

In summary, Maggie Smith's friendships and collaborations within the industry have significantly influenced her career. The bonds she has formed with fellow actors, directors, and writers have not only enriched her artistic journey but also provided a supportive network that has been essential to her success. These relationships, built on mutual respect and shared passion, have left an indelible mark on Smith's life, allowing her to navigate the complexities of the entertainment world with grace and resilience.

Navigating Love and Heartbreak

Maggie Smith's journey through love and heartbreak is a reflection of the complexities that come with balancing a demanding career in the entertainment industry and personal relationships. While her professional life has been marked by remarkable success, her personal experiences have provided a rich tapestry of emotion and growth, shaping her perspective on love and companionship.

After her marriage to Robert Stephens ended, Maggie faced the challenges of navigating single motherhood while pursuing her career. The emotional toll of divorce was palpable, and the stress of balancing her family life with her professional commitments weighed heavily on her. However, she emerged from this challenging period with a renewed sense of purpose and resilience. The experience taught her valuable lessons about love, partnership, and the importance of self-discovery, allowing her to embrace her independence while still cherishing her role as a mother.

In her subsequent relationship with playwright Beverley Cross, Maggie found a deep and meaningful connection that helped to mend the wounds left by her earlier heartbreak. Their marriage was characterized by mutual respect and shared passion for the arts. Cross's support proved invaluable, particularly during moments of uncertainty in Maggie's career. His presence allowed her to feel anchored amidst the pressures of fame, and their partnership flourished, providing a sense of stability that had been missing in her earlier years. However, the heartbreak of losing him to illness in 2008 was a profound challenge for Smith. The grief she experienced during this period was immense, and it served as a poignant reminder of the fragility of love and life.

Despite the pain of loss, Maggie has often spoken about the importance of cherishing memories and maintaining a positive outlook on life. Her ability to navigate the complexities of love and heartbreak speaks to her strength and resilience. Instead of succumbing to despair, she has channeled her emotions into her art, using her experiences as inspiration for her performances. This capacity to transform personal pain into a source of creativity has contributed to her status as a revered actress.

Maggie Smith's perspective on love has also evolved over the years. She has expressed the importance of genuine connections, emphasizing that love should be rooted in respect, understanding, and shared values. Her experiences have led her to appreciate the value of companionship while recognizing that self-love and independence are equally crucial. This balanced approach to love has allowed her to forge meaningful relationships while maintaining a strong sense of self.

Maggie Smith's journey through love and heartbreak is a testament to her resilience and ability to find strength amidst adversity. Her experiences, shaped by both joy and sorrow, have provided her with valuable insights into the nature of love and relationships. Through it all, she has remained committed to her craft, channeling her emotions into her performances and leaving an indelible mark on the entertainment industry. Smith's story serves as an inspiration to many, reminding us that even in the face of heartbreak, love can be a source of growth and transformation.

CHAPTER 4: Health Challenges and Resilience

Struggles with Illness: A Personal Journey

Maggie Smith's journey has not only been defined by her illustrious career but also by the health challenges she has faced throughout her life. These struggles have tested her resilience, shaping her perspective on life and ultimately contributing to her growth as both an actress and an individual. Over the years, Smith has encountered various health issues that have posed significant obstacles, yet her determination to overcome them has become a testament to her strength.

In 2009, Maggie Smith was diagnosed with breast cancer, a moment that marked a turning point in her life. The news was undoubtedly shocking, especially for someone who had dedicated her life to performing. As an actress, Smith had always been in the public eye, and the thought of facing such a personal struggle under the scrutiny of the media added another layer of difficulty. However, she approached her diagnosis with remarkable grace and courage. Rather than allowing the illness to define her, she chose to focus on her treatment and recovery.

Smith underwent surgery and subsequent treatment, which included chemotherapy. Throughout this period, she maintained a strong spirit, finding solace in her work and the support of her family and friends. Despite the physical toll of the treatments, she continued to engage in her craft, demonstrating an unwavering commitment to her career. The experience of battling cancer deepened her appreciation for life and reinforced her understanding of the importance of resilience in the face of adversity.

Her battle with cancer was not just a personal struggle but also a source of inspiration for many. Smith's openness about her diagnosis and journey served to raise awareness about breast cancer and the importance of early detection. She became a role model for those facing similar challenges, showcasing the power of hope and determination. Her story resonated with audiences, reminding them of the strength found in vulnerability.

While her cancer diagnosis was perhaps the most publicized of her health challenges, it was not the only one. Over the years, Smith has faced various other health issues, including a battle with anemia and other age-related ailments. Each of these struggles has presented its own set of challenges, yet she has approached them with the same resilience and determination that characterized her response to cancer. By sharing her experiences, Smith has contributed to the broader conversation about health and aging, helping to destigmatize the challenges that many face as they grow older.

In summary, Maggie Smith's personal journey through illness is marked by courage, determination, and resilience. Her ability to confront health challenges while continuing to pursue her passion for acting has inspired countless individuals. By sharing her story, she has not only raised awareness about critical health issues but also emphasized the importance of maintaining hope and strength in the face of adversity.

Coping Mechanisms and Support Systems

Throughout her life and career, Maggie Smith has developed a range of coping mechanisms and support systems that have helped her navigate the challenges posed by her health issues. Understanding the significance of emotional well-being, she has cultivated a network of support that has been instrumental in her journey, allowing her to face adversities with courage and grace.

One of the key elements of Smith's coping strategy has been her strong family ties. Her sons, Toby and Chris, have been a constant source of support, providing her with love and encouragement during difficult times. Their close-knit relationship has been a pillar of strength for Smith, reminding her of the importance of family bonds in times of adversity. The joy and fulfillment she derives from being a mother have served as a powerful motivator, pushing her to prioritize her health and well-being.

Additionally, friendships within the entertainment industry have played a crucial role in her coping mechanisms. The connections she has forged with fellow actors and colleagues have offered her a sense of community and understanding. Maggie's friendship with Judi Dench is particularly notable, as their shared experiences as actresses have fostered a mutual support system. They have been there for each other through the highs and lows of their careers, providing a listening ear and a shoulder to lean on when needed. These relationships have been invaluable, allowing her to navigate the complexities of her health challenges with a sense of solidarity.

Smith has also found solace in her craft. Acting has long been a form of therapy for her, allowing her to express her emotions and channel her experiences into her performances. Whether on stage or screen, immersing herself in her roles has provided her with an outlet for her feelings, enabling her to cope with her struggles. The act of performing has allowed her to temporarily escape from the realities of her health issues, providing a sense of purpose and fulfillment that contributes positively to her mental well-being.

Moreover, Maggie Smith's resilience can also be attributed to her commitment to self-care. Recognizing the importance of mental and physical health, she has engaged in practices that promote overall well-being. This includes seeking professional help when necessary, embracing mindfulness, and focusing on her nutrition and exercise routines. By prioritizing her health, Smith has empowered herself to face challenges head-on, demonstrating that taking proactive steps can significantly influence one's ability to cope with adversity.

In conclusion, Maggie Smith's coping mechanisms and support systems have been vital in her journey through health challenges. Through strong family bonds, enduring friendships, a commitment to her craft, and proactive self-care, she has demonstrated remarkable resilience. By fostering a network of support and employing effective coping strategies, Smith has managed to navigate her struggles while continuing to inspire others with her strength and determination.

Impact on Career and Public Life

Maggie Smith's health challenges have undeniably influenced her career and public life, shaping not only her personal narrative but also her public persona. The intersection of her health struggles with her work as an actress has had significant implications for her career trajectory, impacting the roles she has chosen, her public image, and her overall approach to her craft.

After her breast cancer diagnosis in 2009, Maggie Smith's approach to her career underwent a subtle yet profound transformation. While she had always been dedicated to her craft, the experience of facing such a serious illness deepened her appreciation for the work she does. This newfound perspective influenced her choices, leading her to embrace roles that resonated with her experiences and emotions. The authenticity she brought to her performances became even more pronounced, allowing her to connect with audiences on a deeper level.

Smith's health challenges also drew public attention, shaping her image as a resilient and courageous figure in the entertainment industry.

Her willingness to share her journey with breast cancer not only raised awareness about the disease but also endeared her to fans and colleagues alike. The public's response was overwhelmingly positive, as many admired her strength in the face of adversity. This connection with her audience contributed to a sense of relatability, allowing her to transcend the boundaries of traditional celebrity status. Rather than being viewed solely as a talented actress, she became a symbol of resilience, inspiring others facing similar health challenges.

While her health struggles brought increased public scrutiny, they also provided Smith with a unique platform to advocate for important causes, particularly those related to women's health and cancer awareness. By using her influence to speak candidly about her experiences, she has contributed to discussions surrounding the importance of early detection and the emotional toll of cancer. This advocacy has not only empowered others but has also solidified her legacy as an actress who is unafraid to address personal challenges.

Despite her health issues, Maggie Smith has continued to pursue her career with vigor. While she has taken breaks to prioritize her health, she has also embraced opportunities that resonate with her, showcasing her enduring passion for acting. Her roles in projects such as "Downton Abbey" and various film adaptations have proven that her talent remains undiminished, despite the challenges she faces. This determination to continue working has reinforced her reputation as a dedicated and passionate artist, inspiring countless individuals within the industry.

Maggie Smith's health challenges have profoundly impacted her career and public life, shaping her narrative as an actress. Through her resilience and willingness to share her experiences, she has cultivated a strong public persona that transcends her roles on screen. By embracing her journey and advocating for important causes, she has left an indelible mark on both her industry and the hearts of her audience, reminding us all of the power of perseverance in the face of adversity.

CHAPTER 5: Later Career and Continued Influence

Iconic Roles in Later Years

Maggie Smith's later career has been marked by a series of iconic roles that not only solidified her status as a legendary actress but also showcased her remarkable versatility and depth. Even as she aged, Smith continued to captivate audiences with her powerful performances, proving that age is no barrier to artistic expression. This period of her career is characterized by significant roles in both film and television that highlight her ability to tackle complex characters with nuance and sensitivity.

One of the standout roles of her later years is that of Professor Minerva McGonagall in the "Harry Potter" film series. From "Harry Potter and the Sorcerer's Stone" to "Harry Potter and the Deathly

Hallows," Smith brought the character to life with her trademark elegance and gravitas. McGonagall, a no-nonsense teacher at Hogwarts School of Witchcraft and Wizardry, became a beloved figure in the franchise, and Smith's portrayal was instrumental in the character's popularity. Her ability to blend authority with warmth resonated with both children and adults, making McGonagall an enduring figure in cinematic history.

In addition to her role in "Harry Potter," Smith garnered widespread acclaim for her performance in the television series "Downton Abbey." Portraying the Dowager Countess Violet Crawley, Smith delivered sharp wit and biting humor, making her character one of the most memorable aspects of the show. The series, which ran from 2010 to 2015, not only earned Smith critical acclaim but also introduced her to a new generation of fans. Her dynamic presence on screen contributed to the show's success, and her ability to convey depth and complexity in a character who is both formidable and endearing won her numerous awards, including three Primetime Emmy Awards.

Moreover, Smith's involvement in prestigious stage productions continued to showcase her theatrical prowess. In 2011, she returned to the West End stage in the play "The Best Exotic Marigold Hotel," based on the hit film. The story revolved around a group of British retirees who travel to India, and Smith's performance as a recently widowed character was lauded for its sensitivity and authenticity. Her portrayal of the character not only demonstrated her range but also highlighted her ability to connect with audiences through emotional storytelling.

As she navigated the later years of her career, Smith also received accolades that celebrated her contributions to the arts. In 2015, she was appointed a Dame Commander of the Order of the British Empire (DBE) for her services to drama, a recognition that cemented her legacy as one of the most revered actresses of her time. This honor not only reflected her remarkable talent but also her commitment to the craft, as she continued to take on challenging roles well into her eighties.

In conclusion, Maggie Smith's later career is characterized by iconic roles that have left a lasting impact on both film and television. Her performances in "Harry Potter" and "Downton Abbey," coupled with her continued contributions to the theatre, have solidified her status as a cultural icon. Through her ability to adapt to diverse characters, Smith has demonstrated that the later stages of one's career can be as impactful and rewarding as the earlier years, inspiring countless actors and actresses around the world.

Contributions to Theatre and Film

Maggie Smith's contributions to theatre and film throughout her career are profound and far-reaching, marking her as a true luminary in the performing arts. With a career that spans several decades, Smith has not only captivated audiences with her performances but has also played a pivotal role in shaping the landscape of both theatre and film. Her commitment to the craft and her ability to tackle diverse roles have left an indelible mark on the industry, inspiring generations of actors.

One of the most significant aspects of Smith's contribution to theatre is her remarkable stage presence. Trained at the prestigious London Academy of Music and Dramatic Art (LAMDA), she honed her skills in live performance, where her ability to connect with audiences became apparent. Smith's work on stage includes a myriad of classic and contemporary plays, where she has portrayed characters ranging from Shakespearean heroines to modern-day figures. Her performances in productions like "A Private Life," "The Changing Room," and "The Importance of Being Earnest" have showcased her versatility and dedication to the theatrical form.

In addition to her performances, Smith has been an advocate for the importance of live theatre. She has often emphasized the unique experience that theatre offers, where the immediacy of live performance allows for a deeper connection between the audience and the actors. Her passion for the stage has encouraged many aspiring actors to pursue careers in theatre, fostering a new generation of talent. Smith's influence can be seen in the way she has championed the importance of storytelling, emphasizing that theatre serves as a vital platform for exploring complex human experiences.

Smith's contributions to film are equally noteworthy. She has participated in a variety of film projects, ranging from acclaimed dramas to light-hearted comedies. Her ability to seamlessly transition between genres has set her apart as a versatile actress. Films such as "The Prime of Miss Jean Brodie" earned her an Academy Award for Best Actress, while her work in "The First Wives

Club" and "The Best Exotic Marigold Hotel" showcased her comedic timing and ability to appeal to a wide audience.

Moreover, Maggie Smith has not only starred in films but has also played a vital role in the evolution of female representation in cinema. Her characters often break traditional molds, offering complex, multi-dimensional portrayals of women. By embracing roles that challenge stereotypes and depict strong, independent female figures, Smith has contributed to the ongoing conversation about gender roles in film. Her legacy is one of empowerment, as she has inspired both female and male actors to explore diverse characters and push the boundaries of traditional storytelling.

As a testament to her contributions, Smith has received numerous accolades throughout her career, including multiple BAFTA Awards, Olivier Awards, and Golden Globe Awards. These honors reflect not only her extraordinary talent but also the impact she has had on the performing arts.

In summary, Maggie Smith's contributions to theatre and film are significant and far-reaching. Her remarkable performances, advocacy for live theatre, and commitment to complex character portrayals have shaped the landscape of the arts. Through her work, Smith has inspired countless actors and audiences, ensuring that her legacy will continue to resonate for generations to come.

Legacy and Influence on New Generations of Actors

Maggie Smith's legacy is one that resonates deeply within the acting community and beyond, influencing new generations of actors who aspire to follow in her footsteps. Her unique blend of talent, resilience, and dedication to her craft has left an indelible mark on the performing arts, shaping not only the roles she has portrayed but also the industry's approach to storytelling and representation.

One of the most significant aspects of Smith's legacy is her ability to transcend generational boundaries. Her performances in iconic films and television series have introduced her to audiences of all ages, creating a sense of familiarity and admiration among aspiring actors. Young performers often cite Smith as a major influence, not only for her exceptional talent but also for her ability to embody complex characters with depth and authenticity. By showcasing a wide range of emotions and experiences, Smith has inspired new actors to explore the intricacies of their craft, encouraging them to delve into the human condition.

Moreover, Smith's commitment to her craft serves as a powerful example for aspiring actors. Throughout her career, she has demonstrated an unwavering dedication to her roles, approaching each character with meticulous attention to detail. This work ethic has set a standard for professionalism within the industry, inspiring younger actors to adopt a similar mindset. Smith's belief in the importance of preparation and rehearsal has been emphasized in various interviews, reinforcing the idea that talent alone is not enough; dedication and hard work are crucial components of success.

Smith's impact extends beyond her performances; she has also been a vocal advocate for the arts and the importance of storytelling. Through her interviews and public appearances, she has often discussed the transformative power of theatre and film, emphasizing the role they play in reflecting society and fostering empathy. By championing the arts, Smith has inspired new generations to recognize the value of their craft, encouraging them to use their platforms to promote social change and address relevant issues.

Additionally, Smith's portrayal of strong, independent female characters has contributed to the evolution of gender representation in the arts. Her roles often challenge traditional stereotypes, showcasing women as multifaceted individuals with their own narratives and complexities. This representation has resonated with aspiring female actors, empowering them to pursue diverse roles that break away from conventional molds. By embodying characters who are unapologetically themselves, Smith has inspired a new wave of actresses to embrace their authenticity and take risks in their careers.

As a result of her influence, many contemporary actors openly express their admiration for Smith and credit her as a source of inspiration. Her legacy can be seen in the performances of younger actors who strive to emulate her ability to convey raw emotion and authenticity. The impact of her career is evident in the storytelling of today, where actors continue to seek roles that push boundaries and challenge societal norms, much like Smith did throughout her own career.

Maggie Smith's legacy and influence on new generations of actors are profound and enduring. Through her remarkable talent, dedication to her craft, and commitment to authentic representation, she has inspired countless individuals to pursue their passions within the performing arts. Smith's contributions continue to shape the industry, ensuring that her impact will be felt for many years to come.

CHAPTER 6: The Narrative of Her Passing

Circumstances Surrounding Her Death

Maggie Smith's passing marked the end of an era in the world of acting and a profound loss for fans, colleagues, and the arts community at large. Smith, who was revered for her talent and grace, passed away at the age of 88. The circumstances surrounding her death were poignant and reflective of the life she had led—a life filled with challenges, triumphs, and an enduring legacy.

In the years leading up to her death, Smith had faced significant health challenges that had affected her ability to work. While she had long been an indomitable presence in the entertainment industry, her health began to decline in her late 80s. Smith had openly spoken about her struggles with illness, including a battle with breast cancer in the late 2000s, which had required surgery and treatment. Despite these obstacles, she remained resilient, often emphasizing her love for acting and her desire to continue performing.

In her final months, Smith spent her time surrounded by family and close friends, focusing on her health and reflecting on her remarkable career. While the details of her final days were kept private, it was known that she had chosen to embrace her life fully, with gratitude for the experiences she had gained and the impact she had made in the world of performing arts. On the day of her passing, she was in the company of loved ones, emphasizing the close relationships she cherished throughout her life.

Smith's death not only marked the loss of a beloved actress but also served as a moment for reflection on her extensive contributions to film, television, and theatre. Her final performances and her influence on future generations of actors became focal points of discussion in the aftermath of her passing, solidifying her status as a cultural icon.

Public Reactions and Tributes

The news of Maggie Smith's death sent shockwaves through the entertainment community and beyond. Tributes poured in from fans, fellow actors, filmmakers, and industry insiders who had been touched by her talent and spirit. Social media became a platform for an outpouring of grief and remembrance, with countless individuals sharing their favorite memories of Smith's performances, her memorable quotes, and the impact she had on their lives.

Prominent actors such as Judi Dench, who had collaborated with Smith on various occasions, expressed their sorrow and admiration in heartfelt statements. Dench described Smith as "a national treasure" and reflected on their friendship, emphasizing the warmth and kindness that defined Smith's character off-screen. Many others in the industry echoed these sentiments, recalling Smith's incredible work ethic, her ability to inspire others, and her generous spirit.

The tribute events that followed her passing showcased not only her extraordinary career but also the love and respect she commanded from her peers. Memorials and retrospectives were organized, featuring screenings of her most iconic films and plays, allowing fans to revisit her remarkable body of work. The British Film Institute and various theatrical organizations paid homage to her contributions, highlighting her pivotal roles and the legacy she left behind.

In the wake of her passing, discussions around Smith's impact on the performing arts intensified. Conversations centered on her role in breaking barriers for women in film and theatre, her influence on younger generations of actors, and the profound emotional resonance of her performances. The loss of Maggie Smith became a rallying point for discussions about the importance of representation, storytelling, and the enduring power of the arts.

Reflection on Her Life and Impact

Maggie Smith's life was a tapestry of achievements, resilience, and artistic brilliance. Reflecting on her journey, it is evident that she was not only an exceptional actress but also a cultural icon whose impact reached far beyond the stage and screen. Smith's dedication to her craft and her ability to connect with audiences made her one of the most beloved figures in the entertainment industry.

Born in 1934 in Essex, England, Smith's early life was marked by a strong passion for acting, nurtured through her education and family support. Her training at the London Academy of Music and Dramatic Art laid the groundwork for a career that would span over six decades. Throughout her life, Smith embraced the challenges of her profession, tackling diverse roles that showcased her range and depth.

Her performances in classic films like "The Prime of Miss Jean Brodie" and her iconic role as Violet Crawley in "Downton Abbey" became benchmarks of excellence in acting. Smith's ability to convey complex emotions and embody multifaceted characters resonated with audiences, leaving an indelible mark on the hearts of many. Her commitment to authenticity in her performances inspired countless actors to approach their craft with the same level of passion and dedication.

Moreover, Smith's advocacy for the arts and her emphasis on storytelling contributed to a broader cultural conversation about the role of performing arts in society. She believed in the transformative power of theatre and film, using her platform to highlight important social issues and champion the importance of representation. Smith's legacy continues to influence the arts, inspiring a new generation of actors to explore the depths of their craft and embrace their unique narratives.

As the world mourns the loss of Maggie Smith, her life serves as a testament to the power of resilience, talent, and grace. Her contributions to the arts will forever be remembered, and her influence will undoubtedly continue to shape the future of acting for generations to come. Through her remarkable journey, Maggie Smith leaves behind not just a legacy of artistic excellence but also a profound reminder of the impact one individual can have on the world through the power of storytelling.

CONCLUSION

Maggie Smith's life and career resonate with brilliance, resilience, and an unwavering commitment to her craft. Her journey, from a young girl discovering her passion for acting in Essex to becoming one of the most respected actresses in the world, exemplifies the power of dedication and artistic expression. Smith's legacy is multifaceted, touching not only her countless fans and admirers but also inspiring generations of actors who seek to follow in her footsteps.

Throughout her illustrious career, Smith graced the stage and screen with her extraordinary talent, bringing a wide array of characters to life. Her ability to transition effortlessly between comedic and dramatic roles showcased her versatility and depth as an actress. From her unforgettable performance in "The Prime of Miss Jean Brodie," which earned her an Academy Award, to her iconic role as the Dowager Countess in "Downton Abbey," Smith captivated audiences with her nuanced portrayals. Each character she portrayed reflected her remarkable range and her skill in imbuing her roles with emotional authenticity.

Smith's contributions extended beyond her performances. She was a trailblazer for women in the entertainment industry, paving the way for future generations to explore and thrive in their artistic endeavors. Her advocacy for the arts and the importance of storytelling left an indelible mark on the industry, encouraging others to use their voices to create meaningful narratives.

As we celebrate her life, it is important to recognize the impact Smith had on the cultural landscape. She transformed the perception of female actors, showcasing their depth and complexity through her diverse roles. Her influence can be seen in the work of many contemporary actresses who cite her as an inspiration. Moreover, the accolades she received—numerous awards, honorary titles, and recognition for her contributions to theatre and film—speak to the respect and admiration she garnered throughout her career.

Maggie Smith's legacy is one of warmth, wisdom, and talent that transcends generations. Her ability to connect with audiences on an emotional level, combined with her philanthropic endeavors and advocacy for the arts, ensures that her influence will continue to resonate long after her passing. In celebrating her life, we honor not just the remarkable actress but also the incredible human being who enriched our lives through her work.

Maggie Smith's journey offers profound lessons that extend far beyond the realm of acting. Her life is a testament to the values of perseverance, authenticity, and the importance of embracing one's passions. These lessons resonate with anyone pursuing their dreams, whether in the arts or any other field.

One of the most significant lessons from Smith's journey is the importance of resilience. Throughout her career, she faced various challenges, including health issues and the ups and downs of the entertainment industry. However, her ability to navigate these obstacles with grace and determination is an inspiring reminder that setbacks do not define us. Instead, it is our response to adversity that shapes our character and determines our success. Smith's refusal to let illness hinder her passion for acting demonstrates the strength of spirit necessary to pursue one's dreams relentlessly.

Moreover, authenticity is a cornerstone of Smith's legacy. She approached her roles with sincerity, bringing her true self into every performance. This dedication to authenticity not only enhanced her portrayals but also established a deep connection with audiences. Smith's ability to convey vulnerability and truth serves as a reminder of the importance of staying true to oneself in a world that often pressures individuals to conform. Her example encourages us to embrace our unique identities and share our authentic selves with the world.

Smith's commitment to her craft and her unwavering love for acting highlight the significance of passion in achieving fulfillment. She once expressed that acting was not merely a profession for her; it was a vital part of her identity. This passion fueled her drive and allowed her to create a remarkable body of work. The lesson here is clear: pursuing what you love is essential to living a fulfilling life. By immersing ourselves in our passions, we can discover our purpose and leave a meaningful impact on the world.

Lastly, Smith's legacy teaches us about the importance of connection and collaboration in the arts. Throughout her career, she formed lasting friendships and partnerships with fellow artists, showcasing the value of community and support in creative endeavors. Her ability to collaborate with diverse talents enriched her work and fostered an environment where creativity could flourish. This highlights the significance of building relationships and engaging with others to enhance our own journeys.

Maggie Smith's life and career offer invaluable lessons that inspire us to embrace resilience, authenticity, and passion while recognizing the power of connection. As we celebrate her legacy, we are reminded that the values she embodied can guide us on our own journeys, encouraging us to pursue our dreams with the same fervor and dedication she exemplified throughout her remarkable life.

Printed in Great Britain
by Amazon